Military
Wheeled Vehicles

by Grace Hansen

MILITARY AIRCRAFT & VEHICLES

abdopublishing.com

Published by Abdo Kids, a division of ABDO, PO Box 398166, Minneapolis, Minnesota 55439.

Copyright © 2017 by Abdo Consulting Group, Inc. International copyrights reserved in all countries. No part of this book may be reproduced in any form without written permission from the publisher.

Printed in the United States of America, North Mankato, Minnesota.

102016

012017

THIS BOOK CONTAINS
RECYCLED MATERIALS

Photo Credits: Images of Freedom, iStock, marines.mil, ©PhotoStock10 p.cover / Shutterstock.com, ©United States Government Work p.5, 17, ©The U.S. Army p.9, 19 / CC-BY-2.0

Production Contributors: Teddy Borth, Jennie Forsberg, Grace Hansen

Design Contributors: Laura Mitchell, Dorothy Toth

Publisher's Cataloging in Publication Data

Names: Hansen, Grace, author.

Title: Military wheeled vehicles / by Grace Hansen.

Description: Minneapolis, Minnesota : Abdo Kids, 2017 | Series: Military aircraft & vehicles | Includes bibliographical references and index.

Identifiers: LCCN 2016944102 | ISBN 9781680809374 (lib. bdg.) | ISBN 9781680796476 (ebook) | ISBN 9781680797145 (Read-to-me ebook)

Subjects: LCSH: Vehicles, Military--Juvenile literature. | Armored vehicles, Military--Juvenile literature.

Classification: DDC 623.7/475--dc23

LC record available at http://lccn.loc.gov/2016944102

Table of Contents

Wheels!

Militaries use wheeled vehicles. Some are used to move soldiers and light cargo. Others are used for **combat**.

4

HMMWVs

HMMWVs have been used by militaries for years. They are also known as Humvees.

7

A Humvee is used to move soldiers and cargo. It is not for fighting on the front lines.

9

A Humvee is lightweight. Its bottom sits high up. It can drive over lots of **terrain**.

Cougars

Cougars are very important
to militaries. They have saved
the lives of many soldiers.

12

A Cougar moves troops
safely through dangerous
battlegrounds. Its V-shaped
bottom protects against mines.

14

Strykers

Strykers are **combat** vehicles. They have eight wheels. They are much lighter than other tanks.

A Stryker can move 60 miles per hour (97 km/h). It gets soldiers quickly to the battlefield. It carries nine soldiers and two crewmembers.

HIMARS

A **HIMARS** is used to strike distant targets. The truck has its weapons mounted on top of it. It launches rockets and missiles to support soldiers on the battlefield.

Cougar 4x4 MRAP Up Close

- Bulletproof and bombproof body

- 6 Passengers: 2 crew 4 troops

- V-shaped support frame

- 2 Hatches (topside)

- 3 Doors

- Top speed:
  65 mph (105 km/h)

- Cruising Range:
  420 mph (676 km/h)

Glossary

combat – armed fighting with enemy forces.

HIMARS – High Mobility Artillery Rocket System.

HMMWV – High Mobility Multipurpose Wheeled Vehicle.

mine – a device containing a charge of explosives.

terrain – a stretch of land, especially with regard to its physical features.

Index

abdokids.com

Use this code to log on to abdokids.com and access crafts, games, videos, and more!

Abdo Kids Code:
MMK9374